CHACO

▨ A CULTURAL LEGACY ▨

Text by
Michele Strutin

■

Photography by
George H. H. Huey

SOUTHWEST PARKS & MONUMENTS ASSOCIATION
TUCSON, ARIZONA

Peñasco ∎
Blanco

WEST MESA

N

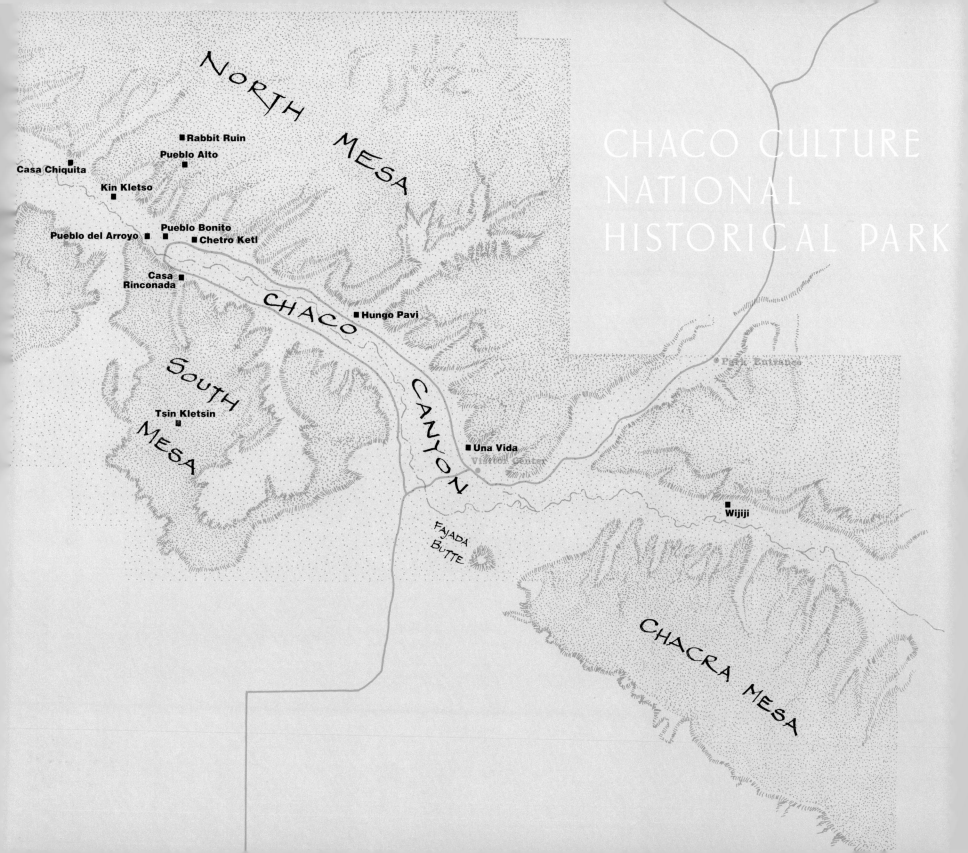

CHACO CULTURE
NATIONAL
HISTORICAL PARK

NORTH MESA

■ Rabbit Ruin

Pueblo Alto ■

Casa Chiquita ■

Kin Kletso ■

Pueblo Bonito
Pueblo del Arroyo ■ ■ ■ Chetro Ketl

Casa
Rinconada ■

CHACO CANYON

■ Hungo Pavi

SOUTH
MESA

Tsin Kletsin ■

■ Una Vida

Visitor Center

Park Entrance

■ Wijiji

FAJADA
BUTTE

CHACRA MESA

Chetro Ketl viewed from
the west, looking down
Chaco Canyon.

CONTENTS

INTRODUCTION

Pottery effigy vessel in the form of a human head.

For six centuries, huge prehistoric buildings lay deserted and undisturbed, buried under sand and silt in a remote canyon in northwestern New Mexico. Now uncovered, these buildings, called "great houses," stand against the sheer north walls of Chaco Canyon, their red-and-ocher sandstone blocks rising four and five stories high, massive even by today's standards.

Many of these great houses, built between the mid-ninth and early twelfth centuries A.D., are older and larger than the famous cliff dwellings at Mesa Verde. In fact, Chaco Canyon contains the largest collection of prehistoric ruins north of Mexico. Until the late nineteenth century, they were the largest buildings in North America.

This was the home of peoples known as the Anasazi and the center of their far-reaching culture. Here men and women worked, children played, and the air was filled with the sound of voices. Religion, trade networks, art—all were part of this Anasazi society. Working with stone tools, Anasazi of the Chaco Canyon area constructed monumental structures, each containing hundreds of rooms. Without benefit of the wheel or beasts of burden, they cut and carried hundreds of thousands of logs for ceilings and lintels from mountain forests at the edge of the horizon.

Now the great houses and other Anasazi structures appear to be all that is left of a populous, ancient society. What happened to these people and, just as puzzling, what drew them to this harsh, arid canyon? At first glance, the area looks too dry to support the fields of corn, beans, and squash that the Anasazi cultivated. Geography holds the answer.

Chaco Canyon lies near the center of the 25,000-square-mile San Juan Basin, a low area on the vast Colorado Plateau. Although little rain falls on the San Juan Basin, much of it drains toward Chaco—just enough to support a canyon society. Viewed from the mesas above Chaco Canyon, the basin's natural boundaries are obvious. Colorado's La Plata and San Juan mountains, many-peaked massifs that rise above the sun-baked mesas and plains, define the northern horizon. To the west and east, respectively, lie the Chuska and Jemez mountains, which resonate with centuries of Native American history and legend. On a clear day, the view of Mount Taylor marks the southern edge of this brittle land.

Today, on the mesas that overlook Chaco Canyon, small herds of cattle and sheep graze on meager grasses. Occasionally a Navajo homestead, with its traditional round hogan and brush corral, breaks the expanse of sagebrush and greasewood. The descent into Chaco reveals a shallow canyon, little more than three hundred feet deep and a mile and a half wide. Chaco Wash, a streambed punctuated by a thin line of

cottonwood trees, bisects the canyon. Average annual precipitation in Chaco is only eight inches, so the wash is usually dry except for brief but furious flooding during spring runoff and summer thunderstorms. The climate today is similar to that in the mid-ninth century, when the Anasazi of the Chaco Canyon area—Chacoans—began building the first great houses.

As elsewhere in the high deserts of the American Southwest, winter temperatures can swiftly plunge below freezing, and biting winds can scour away what little snow might fall. In summer, the sun blazes high in the brilliant blue sky and bakes the dry, dusty land. But this hot, still world can change abruptly. Clouds may appear suddenly, changing in less than an hour from soft, white billows to black fists full of rain. Often veils of rain loosed by these thunderheads evaporate before ever touching the ground. And precipitation can be amazingly local: a brief, cooling thundershower that breaks over Casa Chiquita, in the northwest portion of the park, may never reach the southeastern end of the canyon.

The lack of water limits the kinds of animals living in Chaco. But smaller mammals, such as kangaroo rats, pack rats, prairie dogs, and rabbits are abundant enough to support numerous coyotes and bobcats. At dawn and dusk, cottontails scurry beneath and between the ragged branches of greasewood and four-wing saltbush, tenacious shrubs that dot the canyon floor. Coyotes appear, on the lookout for dinner, and their high-pitched howls and yips echo from the canyon walls.

On the canyon's south side, crumbling cliffs spill fans of broken, eroded rock onto the canyon bottom. At the base of these talus slopes, buried by centuries of silt, lie small villages, some dating back to at least A.D. 700. Although only a few have been excavated, more than three hundred masonry pueblos and storehouses—usually less than a dozen rooms each—line a ten-mile stretch of the central canyon.

Unlike the sloping southern side, the northern canyon walls rise smoothly and abruptly. This sheer, buff-colored sandstone escarpment absorbs and radiates heat from the sun. Here Chacoans chose to construct their expansive great houses. Pueblo Bonito, at the confluence of Chaco Wash and South Gap, was the largest and grandest of the great houses. The immense, D-shaped structure rose four or five stories and was honeycombed with more than 650 rooms and approximately 35 kivas—round rooms that probably served as social and ceremonial spaces. A one-story line of rooms encloses more than three acres of broad plazas at the front of the complex. A short walk to the east lies Chetro Ketl. Almost as big as Pueblo Bonito, Chetro Ketl is noted for its great kiva and its distinctive tower kiva. Its arrow-straight back wall is five hundred feet long.

Chacoan builders were part of a broad civilization that Navajos call Anasazi, meaning "ancient ones," or "ancient ancestors," depending on pronunciation. Anasazi pueblos, kivas, and rock art can be found all over the Colorado Plateau. Mesa Verde, Canyon de Chelly, and the great cliff dwellings at Betatakin and Keet Seel in Navajo National Monument are other significant Anasazi centers. The Anasazi, however, were not the first people to inhabit these lands.

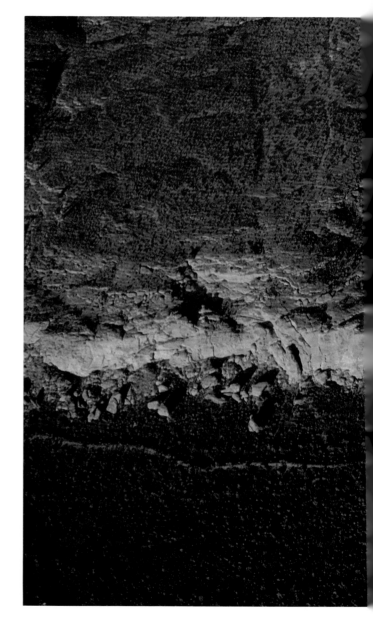

Pueblo Bonito's distinctive D-shape close against the north wall of Chaco Canyon.

e know that ten thousand years ago Paleo-Indians roamed this area, hunting bison and mammals that are now extinct. The earliest evidence of habitation in Chaco Canyon dates back three to four thousand years to what is known as the Archaic period. Bits of basketry, sandals, and seeds dating from that period have been found in Atlatl Cave, which lies at the northwest end of the canyon and was named for the piece of a wooden spear-throwing stick found there. Archaic peoples probably used such atlatls to launch darts, killing small and large mammals that, along with foraged wild plants, formed their diet.

Two to three thousand years ago, these seminomadic hunting-and-gathering groups had begun to experiment with rudimentary farming. Called Basketmaker for the distinctive baskets they wove, they learned to cultivate squash and corn, but had not yet become dependent on an agricultural way of life.

Over the centuries, Basketmaker peoples refined their farming skills and, at the same time, began to develop

9

strains of corn adaptable to the rigors of the San Juan Basin.

Between A.D. 400 and 500, the climate changed, becoming slightly wetter, making it easier to grow crops and, as a result, Chaco Canyon and its environs experienced something of a population boom. Since the late Archaic period, people had been building rudimentary dwellings, digging shallow pits they then roofed with wood, brush, and mud plaster. Basketmaker people added small stone rooms behind these pithouses in which they stored the corn, beans, and squash that had become crucial to their diet.

Grouped together, up to twenty in a cluster, the pithouses and storage rooms eventually became small villages. Shabik'eshchee Village, atop Chacra Mesa at the southeast end of the canyon, is a good example of a sixth-century pithouse village.

By about A.D. 500, the people now termed the early Anasazi had begun living in above-ground, one-story masonry dwellings built around a central pithouse. This evolution from hunter-gatherers to pithouse dwellers to agricultural communities living in attached, multifamily pueblos occurred

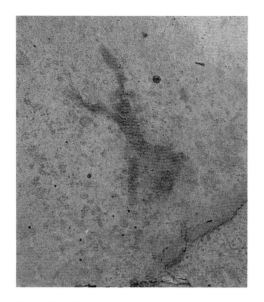

Basketmaker-era pictograph, red ocher on sandstone.

Stairway near Casa Rinconada, typical of those found throughout the canyon.

throughout the Southwest. But what happened next at Chaco Canyon was so dramatically different that archeologists have termed it the Chaco Phenomenon.

Beginning in the mid-ninth century, the Anasazi of the Chaco Canyon area began to transform moderately sized arc-shaped pueblos into the great houses of the central canyon. Over the next 250 years, Chacoans built dozens of great houses in and around Chaco Canyon, including Pueblo Bonito, Chetro Ketl, Una Vida, Pueblo del Arroyo, Hungo Pavi, Kin Kletso, Casa Chiquita, Peñasco Blanco, and Pueblo Alto.

Chacoans also carved stairways into cliffsides so they could travel more easily between the great houses and the mesas. They created irrigation structures in order to catch runoff that spilled off the cliffs during thunderstorms and channel it into gridded farm plots. And the pithouse of Basketmaker times evolved into the kiva.

Chacoans supplemented basketry with coiled pottery vessels of every shape and purpose, decorated with intricate and artistic geometric designs whose beauty has not aged. They produced gorgeous turquoise jewelry as well as polished bone scrapers and other implements inlaid with semi-precious stones. The living areas of Chacoan great houses were often plastered and painted. Copper bells, shells, and macaw remains found in the great houses probably arrived at Chaco along trade routes that reached flourishing Mesoamerican cultures in what is now northern Mexico.

Among the most intriguing aspects of the Chaco Phenomenon is a road system radiating from Chaco Canyon and totaling hundreds of miles. Some of these roads are as wide as thirty feet and more than forty miles long, and lead to or are associated with outlying great houses. More than a hundred of these outlying communities are located all over the Colorado Plateau.

No one knows how many Anasazi looked to Chaco as the center of their world, but some archeologists suspect many traveled there as pilgrims, swelling the canyon's permanent population.

The Chaco Phenomenon represented a startling burst of activity. From the late ninth century to the mid-twelfth century, the Chacoan Anasazi developed a complex society that built massive structures and influenced life through-out the Colorado Plateau and beyond. Yet, by A.D. 1150 Chaco Canyon and its buildings were virtually deserted.

Scientists know that the Anasazi who inhabited Chaco did not disappear. Apparently, some even returned to Chaco for a period during the 1200s. Over time, most of the population likely moved west to the Chuska Mountains and Hopi region or to join the Mesa Verde Anasazi to the north. Ultimately, many Anasazi departed for areas along more stable water courses. Today, Puebloan people consider the Anasazi their ancestors.

In the quest for answers about the Chaco Phenomenon, archeologists have advanced from crude and large-scale excavations at the turn of the century to more sophisticated and less invasive techniques. The emphasis, too, has shifted from unearthing treasures to preserving what remains of this culture for future generations. In recognition of its significance, Chaco has been designated as both a national historical park and a World Heritage site.

Like any good detective story, Chaco offers many clues. But the final chapter of the Chaco story has yet to be written, and the earlier chapters are continually being revised. In the end, Chaco may never reveal all of its secrets.

Scraping tool made of bone, inlaid with jet and turquoise.

**Painting of Pueblo
Pintado by Richard Kern,
Simpson's expedition,
1849.**

In August 1849, a United States Army expedition set out from Fort Marcy in Santa Fe and headed west to suppress Navajo raids against ranchers in New Mexico. Traveling along the northern flank of Chacra Mesa, the column came upon large ruins. Carravahal, a guide from the town of San Ysidro, was reputed to know every distinctive feature in that part of the Southwest.

He called the ruin Pueblo Pintado ("Painted Village"), probably for the vestiges of painted plaster found there. Lieutenant James H. Simpson, an engineer assigned to survey the area, found the land bleak and featureless. To him, Pueblo Pintado was a revelation. He wrote:

It discovers in the masonry a combination of science and art which can only be referred to a higher stage of civilization and refinement than is discoverable in the works of Mexicans or Pueblos of the present day. Indeed, so beautifully diminutive and true are the details of the structures as to cause it, at a little distance, to have all the appearance of a magnificent piece of mosaic work.

One of Simpson's assistants, artist and cartographer Richard Kern, was also impressed. He sketched Pueblo Pintado against a cloud-splattered sky, with the same sort of brooding majesty found in contemporary paintings of Roman or Greek ruins. Simpson carefully detailed the pueblo, noting it had fifty-four ground-floor rooms and was probably three stories high.

The expedition entered Chaco Canyon, but Simpson and members of the survey team let the others go on ahead of them. Intrigued by their discovery, they wanted to take their time exploring the series of ruins they had encountered.

Though shrouded with centuries of sediment, each group of ruins was successively grander—Wijiji, Una Vida,

OPPOSITE—**Pueblo Pintado.**

Hungo Pavi, Chetro Ketl, Pueblo del Arroyo, and Pueblo Bonito. Exiting the canyon at its confluence with Escavada Wash, Simpson was delighted by Pueblo de Peñasco Blanco, which lies on a bench of land above the wash. The precision of beams and doorways, the round kivas, and the sherds of pottery all fascinated him. He noted the elegant work: layers of large stones alternated with courses of finely cut stone to create the mosaic look he admired.

Simpson's report stirred speculation. Some believed Aztecs had built the Chacoan great houses. Simpson personally thought they were the work of the Toltecs. Few thought that ancestors of indigenous Puebloan peoples could have conceived or built anything with such craft and on such a scale.

To Simpson, Chaco was evidence of a once-vital civilization now abandoned in a vacant place. The ruins of Chaco Canyon lay like Shelly's Ozymandias: "Round the decay of that colossal wreck, boundless and bare the lone and level sands stretch far away." But Simpson's enthusiastic report evinced little official interest in Washington, D.C.

The next significant exploration of Chaco occurred in 1877. That year,

The Jackson Stairs can be seen from the Pueblo Alto Trail.

OPPOSITE—**Kin Kletso, photographed by Victor Mindeleff.**

Narrowleaf yucca and Indian paintbrush.

photographer William Henry Jackson, who was attached to the famous Hayden surveys of the western United States, mapped and described the pueblos Simpson had seen twenty-eight years earlier. Guided by Hosta, governor of Jemez Pueblo, the photographer located Kin Kletso, Casa Chiquita, and Pueblo Alto, a great house on Alto Mesa that he named for its elevation and dramatic view. Jackson also discovered several stairways cut into the sheer, smooth sandstone cliffs. One such stairway, which ascends near Chetro Ketl to Alto Mesa, is now called the Jackson Stairs.

Jackson's most provocative contribution, however, was more anthropological. Having spent time with the Hopis, Jackson saw the connection between these Puebloan people and the sites he explored in Chaco. He believed Chaco was most likely built by indigenous Puebloan people and not by Toltecs, Aztecs, or any other Meso-american culture.

Soon, other photographers, ethnographers, magazine writers, and archeologists began making trips to Chaco. In the late 1880s, Victor and Cosmos Mindeleff, of the American Bureau of Ethnography, compared their

photographs of Chacoan architecture with photographs of functioning nineteenth-century pueblos. The comparison supported the idea that Chacoan great houses were the work of an ancient but indigenous people.

In 1896, the Hyde Exploring Expedition, mounted by Richard Wetherill and financed by Talbot and Frederick Hyde of New York, heirs to a soap fortune, ushered in an era of excavation. One of a pioneering ranching family, Wetherill had roamed much of the Colorado Plateau looking for—and finding—archeological sites. He was the first to popularize the Navajo term Anasazi, and also coined the term Basketmaker for the people he believed preceded the Anasazi.

Asked to provide scientific leadership, the director of the American Museum of Natural History sent George Pepper, a twenty-three-year-old student. Wetherill, Pepper, and a crew of Navajo laborers spent the next four summer seasons uncovering Chaco, with Pueblo Bonito as their focus.

During the first season they cleared thirty-seven of Pueblo Bonito's rooms. After removing dirt and debris with picks and shovels, they turned to

Pottery cache discovered in Pueblo Bonito during the Hyde expedition.

The Wetherill Trading Post at Pueblo Bonito, 1898.

smaller implements to unearth artifacts. Each item was described as to its location in the room, and each room was mapped, photographed, and numbered.

After surveying a room and removing valuable artifacts, they usually backfilled it with dirt excavated from the next room. This backfilling inadvertently helped preserve the rooms for future, more sophisticated archeology. Nineteenth-century excavators were not as fastidious about preservation as are today's archeologists. For instance, some archeologists used materials from excavations to build their own dwellings.

At so dramatic a ruin as Pueblo Bonito, the Hyde expedition expected to make dramatic discoveries, and they were not disappointed. One room alone was filled with a cache of 114 pottery jars and 18 pitchers decorated with bold black-and-white geometric designs. Elsewhere, they found a quiver containing eighty-one arrows, several hundred pieces of carved wood that probably served as prayer sticks, and polished deer-bone scrapers inlaid with jet and turquoise. They found flutes, stone effigies of birds and frogs inlaid with turquoise and shells, and yucca-fiber sandals. Another find, a heavy basket, was decorated with a mosaic of turquoise and filled with thousands of turquoise and shell beads and nearly two hundred turquoise pendants. Some of the jewelry and artful figures were found in rooms surmised to be burial chambers of apparently high-ranking members of Chacoan society.

At the end of the first season, the artifacts shipped back to the American Museum of Natural History in New York filled a railroad freight car. By the end of the fourth season, the Hyde expedition had excavated 190 rooms and kivas at Pueblo Bonito. The museum's 1901 itemization listed fifty thousand pieces of turquoise, ten thousand pieces of pottery, five thousand stone implements, one thousand bone and wood artifacts, some fabric, copper bells, and a few conch-shell horns.

Although Pepper's record-keeping on the digs was extensive and precise, his anthropological interpretation was light. The origins of copper bells and conch shells were a mystery, but Pepper guessed that the quantities of turquoise came from Los Cerillos, a mining site used for centuries and located near present-day Santa Fe. His reports were not published for two decades, but in them Pepper, like Jackson, noted similarities between the inhabitants of Chaco and Puebloan people of his own time.

From the start, Wetherill had been trading informally with the laborers and other Navajos living in the area. In 1898 he opened a one-room trading post, built against the back wall of Pueblo Bonito. He eventually enlarged it to a three-room structure: one room housed the Wetherills, one room was Pepper's, and the third was a trading post, which drew Navajos from all over the region to trade jewelry, woven rugs, and

Chacoan cylinder jars, apparently unique, pottery forms.

17

blankets for provisions. The trading post proved so successful that the Wetherill family eventually established a chain of them.

As findings of the Hyde Exploring Expedition became known around the country, other scientists came to carry out smaller-scale explorations. Pot-hunters began showing up as well. There were reports of stolen artifacts and vandalized sites. The amount of commerce and activity concerned academics, especially the University and Museum of New Mexico's Dr. Edgar Hewett, later an important figure in Chaco research. Eventually, Congress got involved.

In 1900, Land Office Agent S.J. Holsinger was assigned to investigate. In addition to statements from members of the Hyde expedition, his report contained accounts of everything he saw in the canyon, and the first accurate survey of the natural surroundings. Holsinger's report also was the first to note other significant Anasazi struc-tures in and near the canyon: Casa Rinconada, Tsin Kletzin, Kin Klizhin, Kin Bineola, and Kin Ya'a.

Holsinger noted evidence of irriga-tion systems—dams, reservoirs, and

ditches—and analyzed how many acres of land the Anasazi could have irrigated. In addition to the rock stairs found by Jackson, Holsinger reported the remains of an ancient roadway that connected Chetro Ketl in the canyon with Pueblo Alto atop Alto Mesa.

He wondered about the huge timbers that supported the roofs of Chaco's great kivas. Trees that big and that numerous did not grow around Chaco, and carrying a quarter- to half-ton timber must have been a terrific undertaking for people whose feet served as the only means of transportation. Researchers estimate that more than two hundred thousand large and small timbers were used at Chaco. Holsinger believed that some of the logs had been carried from as far as sixty miles away.

His greatest attention, however, was reserved for Pueblo Bonito, which he called the "ruin of ruins, the equal of which in point of magnitude and general interest, is not to be found among the world's collection of discovered prehistoric structures." He noted the graceful, sweeping curve of the pueblo and the finely formed doors and windows. Like Simpson, he ad-

Detail of roof construction, Pueblo del Arroyo.

OPPOSITE—**Pueblo Bonito.**

Petroglyph of six-toed feet. Their significance is unknown.

mired the mosaic effect of the masonry. Holsinger's reports on the commercial activities at Chaco hastened the end of the Hyde expedition.

Mounting concerns about unregulated activity at archeological sites led Congress to pass the 1906 Antiquities Act to protect historic and prehistoric sites on public lands. Protection for Chaco Canyon came the following year, when President Theodore Roosevelt signed legislation designating Chaco Canyon National Monument. Thus, Chaco became a nationally protected area nine years before the creation of the National Park Service. In the interim, a Navajo trader served as caretaker.

After the Hyde Exploring Expedition disbanded, interest in Chaco again waned. In 1916, only a hundred people visited. The canyon was still a two- to three-day journey from Farmington, New Mexico, and outfitters could provide only makeshift camps.

Meanwhile, the body of knowledge about the Anasazi was growing as researchers explored Aztec Ruins, Betatakin, and other southwestern sites. This research helped fill gaps in the archeological record of Basketmaker and other early periods.

Neil Judd, curator of archeology at the new United States National Museum (now part of the Smithsonian Institution), in 1921 embarked on the first federally authorized archeological excavation in Chaco Canyon. Judd, who had already discovered and described a number of Anasazi sites, set out to explore Pueblo Bonito and Pueblo del Arroyo specifically. The Judd expedition, funded by the National Geographic Society, lasted until 1927 and members of the expedition worked from four to six months each season. Navajos and Zunis were employed as laborers; other staff included a geologist, truck driver, cook, photographer, surveyor, an architectural draftsman, and archeology graduate students who served as field assistants.

At the beginning of his quest, Judd announced his goals in a *National Geographic* magazine article: "This expedition hopes to discover the historic secrets of a region which was one of the most densely populated areas in North America before Columbus came, a region where prehistoric peoples lived in vast communal dwellings whose ruins are ranked second to none of ancient times."

Judd's approach to excavation differed from those of his predecessors. He believed the buildings themselves, as much as the artifacts they contained, were national treasures that should lay open to the public. Instead of back-filling, his crew carted away tons of excavated sediment and rubble in horse-drawn wagons and mule-drawn ore carts—an enormously time-consuming, labor-intensive operation.

The Judd team also maintained a more enlightened preservation ethic than previous excavators. They did not punch holes in masonry in order to reach lower levels. They removed wood-beam ceilings to get at rooms below, but unlike earlier excavators, who burned the wood for fuel, Judd's team saved the beams to be analyzed using the newly developed science of dendrochronology. After removing mountains of debris, which had helped to stabilize the masonry structures, Judd's crew began patching masonry, replacing lintels, and strengthening walls. At Pueblo Bonito, they excavated an additional 138 rooms plus 24 kivas, including 2 great kivas, which are grander than typical kivas both in size and style. He estimated the pueblo contained a total of 651 rooms.

Like those before him, Judd was struck by the magnitude of the buildings in Chaco Canyon. Referring to Pueblo Bonito in a later article for *National Geographic*, he wrote, "No other apartment house of comparable size was known in America or in the Old World until the Spanish Flats were erected in 1882 at Fifty-ninth Street and Seventh Avenue, New York City."

Judd estimated that, at its height between the eleventh and twelfth centuries, Pueblo Bonito may have housed as many as a thousand people. If Chaco's buildings were all occupied as large, crowded apartment buildings, the canyon would have seemed an urban place—indeed, one of the great population centers of North America at that time. But could the environment have supported so many?

In order to answer such questions, archeologists turned to evolving techniques. By the 1920s, they had refined their use of stratigraphy, a technique for learning about a culture by examining successive strata of trash. The sequence of pottery development in the Southwest and its association with certain peoples and certain areas was becoming clear. Judd hoped that trashed pottery sherds would be his key to understanding Chaco.

As Anasazi culture developed, so had their pottery: from early, shaped pieces to vessels made of stacked coils, then smoothed, painted, and fired. Archeologists can identify the period during which a piece of pottery was made by the types of paints, designs, and clays the potter used. Even within a time period, archeologists can usually determine whether a pot was made by people living near the Chuska Mountains, for example, or Mesa Verde.

The Judd team cut away two sections of Pueblo Bonito's trash pile, or midden, but could make no sense of what they found. Instead of finding the oldest materials at the bottom of the heap, as would be expected, early-style sherds were found near the top, while newer pottery fragments were buried near the bottom. In 1924, the mystery was solved. The team found that the oldest segment of Pueblo Bonito was its northwest corner. The original midden stood in the way of new construction, so Chacoan builders simply removed the early waste and dumped it on top of a newer midden.

In addition to stratigraphy, Judd used dendrochronology, or tree-ring dating, to help chart the sequence of prehistoric times. Each year, trees add a concentric growth ring. In wet years, the ring is wider; in dry years, it is narrower. Painstakingly, researchers have built a master chart of this narrow-wide pattern stretching back more than two thousand years of southwestern history. By comparing the ring patterns of a particular kiva beam in Pueblo Bonito with the master chart, scientists can determine the cutting date to a specific year.

Similarly, Judd also began grouping Chacoan culture into periods according to the attributes of its masonry. Using this technique, he concluded that Pueblo Bonito began much like any pueblo village: a simple semicircle of masonry rooms centered on a kiva. By the time Pueblo Bonito was completed, it was fifty times larger than this original structure, and had evolved to meet the needs of a far more complex society.

Most of the rock used in Bonito Phase masonry, at the height of Chacoan architecture, was quarried

■ High-Tech Detection

Tree-ring dating is still one of the most accurate ways to date wood, but it does not work well for fiber and other organic materials. For these, radiocarbon dating is often used. The carbon-14 isotope, found in all organic material, loses its radioactivity over a period of 5,568 years. By measuring the radioactivity remaining in a sample, its age can be determined.

Archeomagnetism is used to date soil that has been heated to high temperatures, such as adobe mud used in constructing Chacoan fire hearths. When heated, the iron molecules in the clay align with magnetic north. The movement of the magnetic North Pole over the centuries has been charted, so the "pole" from a sample can be matched with the chart to determine the firing date.

Even rodents play a role in dating Chacoan culture. Packrats build their nests using locally gathered materials, including bits of pottery, grain, and twigs. At Chaco, scientists have sampled numerous packrat middens, some of which have been occupied by countless generations dating back ten thousand years. By slicing through middens and carbon dating samples, archeologists have found seeds and pollen from five to ten thousand years ago. These studies show that just before the rise of Chacoan culture, the land was much as it is now except there were more pinyon pine and one-seed juniper. Pinyon pollen dramatically decreases in packrat middens when Chacoan culture was at its height, and reappears after Chaco was abandoned. Some archeologists suspect that Chacoan builders may have stripped the surrounding land of trees for construction material and fuel by the late eleventh century.

from a layer of dense, dark sandstone that capped the cliffs just behind the Chacoan great houses. Once quarried, it was probably dropped to the canyon floor where it would be shaped and dressed.

As the team uncovered more of the Chacoan puzzle, they discovered that the builders of Pueblo Bonito had no compunction about filling in and covering over old spaces with new rooms and kivas. Judd also found evidence that thin layers of plaster had covered Chacoan walls, although a millennium of wind and water had stripped most of them away. The walls of many plaster-clad rooms had been painted with bands of color, usually red or white.

Judd made one discovery whose beauty impressed him all his life. Coiled between two floor stones lay a four-strand turquoise necklace and two pendant earrings. The cords holding the 2,500 beads together had disintegrated, but the team was able to restring the delicately wrought beads on a laborer's fine-gauge banjo string.

For the most part, however, Judd's findings were the mundane stuff of daily life, and they helped piece together a more comprehensive and representative picture of Chacoan existence. As Judd himself said about his work, "The chief recompense is the satisfaction one derives from adding a few sentences to the world's history, in contributing even a short paragraph to the story of human progress."

His findings present a picture of Pueblo Bonito as a smoothly plastered pueblo stepped so that each story opened onto a terrace formed by the roof of the story below. Ladders of lashed-together poles afforded access to upper levels, and down into the circular kivas. Rooms that opened onto the terraces contained tools and furnishings while the dark, often featureless rooms behind were more likely used to store corn, squash, and beans, which formed the base of Chacoans' cultivated foods.

Judd found no evidence of movable furniture, but he did find plenty of reed mats, probably used for sleeping, as well as woven blankets and turkey-feather robes. Sleeping platforms, pegs for clothing and bedclothes, and cupboard-like niches in the masonry formed the extent of room furnishings. Most likely, much of Chacoans' time was spent outside, tending agricultural plots, hunting, building or repairing

A four-strand turquoise necklace and pendants excavated by Neil Judd in Pueblo Bonito in the 1920s.

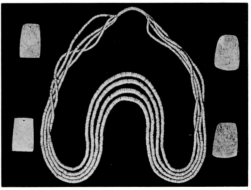

structures, and making pottery on the terraces. Chacoan women likely worked for hours each day grinding corn into flour. They used loaf-shaped stones, or *manos,* to grind the corn in stone troughs called *metates.* Judd found six metates lined up in a row of rooms facing Bonito's huge courtyard.

Judd did not envision Chaco as a place apart, where men hoed their rows of corn with little cognizance of a larger world. For one thing, he believed that Chaco was part of a far-reaching turquoise trade, perhaps starting from the mine at Los Cerillos and encompassing the Pacific coast and the civilizations of northern Mexico.

He found evidence that Chaco Canyon supported stands of trees during the period it was populated. That, plus the number of excavated rush mats, led him to believe that Chaco must have received more precipitation in prehistoric times. He believed, however, that Chacoans eventually were forced to go farther afield for building timbers. He also thought that the Chacoans might have cut down so many of the trees and farmed the land so intensively that they used up their available resources and had to abandon

the canyon. One thing puzzled Judd: For the number of rooms excavated in Pueblo Bonito, they found few human burials—so few that he could not make the number of burials correspond with the population he would have expected to find in the great house.

Forty years after Judd completed these excavations, he finally published the results of his work. Although not all of his suppositions were correct, he did try to examine the larger picture of Chaco Canyon. And years after he had completed his work, Judd was still awed by this flowering of civilization in the desert.

Frog of highly polished jet inlaid with turquoise *(actual size).*

A few years after Judd's National Geographic excavations ended, researchers began exploring other significant archeological features in the canyon, beginning with Pueblo Bonito's neighbor, Chetro Ketl. In 1929 and for the next eight seasons, Edgar Hewett led a team representing the cooperative efforts of the Museum of New Mexico, the School of American Research, and the University of New Mexico. This effort also sparked the careers of other Chaco researchers, such as Florence Hawley Ellis, whose dendrochronology charts greatly advanced the chronology of Chacoan civilization. Another was Gordon Vivian, who became the National Park Service's lead archeologist in preserving and restoring Chaco as part of the national park system.

Like Pueblo Bonito, Chetro Ketl is a huge, D-shaped edifice rising about four stories. Unlike Pueblo Bonito, Chetro Ketl's curved section is the arc of rooms that encloses the pueblo's enormous, elevated courtyard. Although Pueblo Bonito contains more building mass, Chetro Ketl encloses a larger area totalling about three and a half acres.

Shell and stone necklace,
about sixteen feet long,
excavated during the
Hyde expedition.

Hewett estimated it took fifty million pieces of stone and more than five thousand trees to construct the pueblo. With huge sandstone cliffs backing Chetro Ketl, it was easy to guess where the stone was quarried. Nearby prehistoric forests were not extensive, so the origin of thousands of tree trunks was baffling. The colonnade fronting Chetro Ketl plaza was another puzzle. This covered porch, supported by pillars, is the only such structure in Chaco.

When Hewett and his team began excavating Chetro Ketl's courtyard they found that the seemingly flat expanse was underlain by kivas of all sizes and from all periods of Chacoan construction. The most significant was Chetro Ketl's great kiva, some sixty feet in diameter with a broad masonry bench circling its inner walls, a feature typical to all kivas.

The researchers also found features unique to great kivas, including a masonry fire box flanked by two rectangular vaults. In addition, four masonry-lined pits form a square on the floor of the great kiva. Each pit is paved with a half-ton sandstone disc on which rested a giant timber. These timbers, each about two feet in diameter, supported the kiva's massive roof and the discs kept the timbers from settling into

the ground. The kiva's roof was like that of most Chacoan rooms: a series of beams laid next to one another, covered by willow matting, brush, then dirt. The Anasazi entered regular kivas via a roof hatch and a ladder. In this great kiva, a set of stone stairs lead down from a northern antechamber on the plaza.

Hewett found twenty-nine open, empty niches spaced around the circular kiva walls. The great kiva lies atop an older, smaller great kiva in which Hewett found ten sealed niches. These held ritual objects: turquoise pendants and necklaces, some as much as seventeen feet long, made with thousands of stone and shell beads.

These specific discoveries and Chacoan civilization, in general, were put into perspective by Florence Hawley Ellis's exacting dendrochronological work at Chetro Ketl. Using pieces of charcoal and timber found in the great house as material for tree-ring dating, Ellis constructed a guide to Chacoan building periods. Stratigraphy of Chacoan trash dumps also allowed Ellis to match charcoal dates to pottery sherds found in the same layer, creating a chronology for Chaco's pottery as well.

Ellis classified the first building

▣ Crafting the Roof

The roofs of great kivas were massive. For instance, the roof of the great kiva at Aztec Ruins is estimated to have weighed ninety-five tons. Roofs this big needed interior support. Thus, four giant upright logs stood in huge masonry pits that formed a quadrangle near the center of the kiva floor. The logs, as much as twelve feet high, served as supports for timbers laid horizontally across the top. Great kivas, as well as numerous smaller kivas, had flat roofs.

Far more common were kivas with cribbed roofs. Cribbed-roof construction started with six to eight low, masonry bases built on top of the bench encircling the kiva. Long logs were laid between the masonry bases. Then Chacoan builders layered successive tiers of slightly shorter logs upward like the crown of a beehive until they reached the desired ceiling height. At the top they left a hole that served as both smokehole and kiva entrance. The log cribbing created a domed ceiling whose intricate pattern of tiered timbers must have looked elegant in the firelight. From the outside, the cribbing was invisible because the open space between the circular kiva walls and the dome-shaped cribbing was filled with earth. Thus, the roof of a cribbed kiva appeared as a flat surface to those in the plaza above.

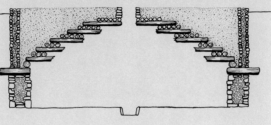

Kiva with cribbed roof.

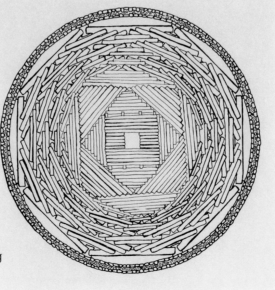

period at Chetro Ketl from A.D. 945 to 1030. During these years, Chaco builders used Type II core-and-veneer construction. During the next period, 1030 to 1090, the core-and-veneer masonry style was further refined and the art of Chacoan pottery, with its polished black-on-white designs, reached its peak.

The third and last period classified by Ellis was a brief eighteen years, from 1099 to 1117. The quality of masonry had degenerated and the last wood date Ellis found in all of Chetro Ketl was from 1116. For about 175 years, life at Chetro Ketl had flourished, then—nothing. Sometime during the early part of the twelfth century, this great house, like all the others at Chaco, was deserted.

Until the 1930s, research at Chaco had concentrated on the great houses. Under Hewett's direction, archeologists turned their attention to a monumental structure along Chaco Canyon's south side. At 63.5 feet in diameter, Casa Rinconada is the largest known great kiva in the canyon. But Casa Rinconada does not lie alone. Of the three hundred small houses that line the canyon's south side, a cluster of excavated small houses lie near Casa Rinconada. Researchers are now certain that the small houses were inhabited at the same time as the great houses, and one idea is that Casa Rinconada may have served as a ceremonial link between the two sides of the canyon.

As in the great kivas at Pueblo Bonito and Chetro Ketl, the inner walls of Casa Rinconada are circled by a masonry bench. Above the bench are spaced thirty-four niches, which were open and empty when the kiva was excavated. A fire box, floor vaults, a north stairway entrance, and stone-lined pits that held enormous timbers supporting the twelve-foot-high ceiling are, again, standard features. A second set of stairs on the south side descends into the kiva from a ground-level antechamber.

Casa Rinconada's most unusual feature lies at the north, where side rooms flank a two-room antechamber and the stone steps that lead into the kiva. Hidden beneath the steps lies another stairway leading down into an arcing, stone-lined trench in the kiva floor that may have been screened by poles. Some archeologists believe this hidden entrance allowed religious

The great kiva at Casa Rinconada is aligned precisely with celestial north.

Cliff rose.

leaders to make dramatic, "magical" entrances into the kiva during ceremonies.

The kiva's rectangular masonry floor vaults may also have been used ceremonially. Judging from modern Puebloan usage, some archeologists surmise that plank-covered vaults may have served as foot drums, echoing rhythmically with the sounds of ritual dance. Corn, bean, and squash sprouts used in rituals may have been grown in these vault "planters" as well.

Astronomical alignment may be another aspect of Chacoan ceremony. For instance, although most great kivas are generally aligned north-south, Casa Rinconada is aligned precisely with celestial north. In addition, some researchers see evidence that an opening in the northeastern wall and a niche on the kiva's western side may be aligned so that a shaft of sunlight filled the niche with light at sunrise on the summer solstice. Others argue that peripheral rooms around the kiva or the northwest roof support post would have blocked the light. Regardless, the Anasazi often used celestial markers as guides for aligning buildings and other structures.

How the Anasazi used their kivas

The great kiva at Pueblo Bonito.

remains a subject of supposition. Scientists think smaller kivas may have been used by extended families or clans as combination work rooms and ceremonial centers. Great kivas were probably used for religious-civic ceremonies.

By the mid-1930s, researchers had learned much about Chaco, but had also run into a few problems. The National Park Service, the University of New Mexico, and the School of American Research, plus trading-post owners and private landowners, were all squabbling about rights, laws, and who could do what where. Over the next decade, most questions of ownership were worked out, and it became clear that archeological study at Chaco should be organized under a single agency.

From 1947 on that agency has been the National Park Service. That year Gordon Vivian was named head of archeology for the park and, under his leadership, archeologists began testing portions of Pueblo del Arroyo and other sites as part of an overall preservation effort. Their findings expanded what was known about Chacoan civilization and at the same time added questions and complexity.

At Pueblo del Arroyo, archeologists excavated a structure with three concentric, circular walls. This tri-wall construction, unique for Chaco Canyon, was similar to structures archeologists had found at Aztec Ruins and in the Mesa Verde area.

The architecture of Kin Kletso, excavated during Vivian's tenure, and Casa Chiquita also looked more Mesa Verdean than Chacoan. Rooms and kivas fit into a compact, rectilinear structure and neither has an enclosed plaza. The masonry lacks the curved lines and elegant mosaic effect of Pueblo Bonito's walls. Also, the sandstone slabs are much larger, softer, and lighter in color. Archeologists call this blocky style "McElmo," after a ruin-filled canyon in the Mesa Verde area, a hundred miles north of Chaco.

Tree-ring dates show that Kin Kletso was built in the early twelfth century, near the end of Chaco's most architecturally productive period, and just before Chacoan construction came to an end. Stone for these later pueblos likely was quarried from the softer sandstone near the base of the cliffs. Archeologists believe that, by the last quarter of the eleventh century, most of the dark, dense stone used for classic Chacoan buildings had been virtually stripped from the rim of the cliffs.

Discovery was not Gordon Vivian's only focus. Under his leadership, Chaco preservation and stabilization techniques improved considerably. All buildings require maintenance, particularly those that are a thousand years old and have no roofs or protective plaster. Park staff strengthened mud mortar with a variety of additives, built unobtrusive dikes to divert flash floods, and improved drainage within the pueblos as part of the ongoing preservation effort. During this period, trading posts and early field stations were dismantled and, in 1957, a modern, fully staffed park visitor center opened.

By the 1960s, archeologists had amassed an incredible amount of information about Chaco. Yet, knowledge about Chacoan society was about to take a quantum leap with the beginning of the Chaco Project.

CHAPTER TWO

ROADS, WATER, & HOUSEHOLDS

In 1971, a new era in research at Chaco began with the start of the Chaco Center. Established by the National Park Service, in conjunction with the University of New Mexico, the Chaco Center's goal was to achieve a comprehensive view of the archeological sites at Chaco Canyon. Robert Lister was the first director of the Chaco Center. He was followed by James Judge, who led the Center for the second half of its ten-year life.

Before the Chaco Center was established, archeologists had focused on describing or excavating a few structures. The early archeologists did not have the sophisticated tools or the numbers of people to piece together a more comprehensive picture of Chacoan life and how it fit into the larger world. The Chaco Project, as it was called, aimed for nothing less.

To pick-and-shovel archeology researchers added a full spectrum of high-tech tools that would put work at Chaco on the cutting edge of archeology. Chacoan ruins, among the largest and best preserved, yet most inexplicable in the country, were ideal subjects

Cluster of spiral petroglyphs.

Pictograph near Peñasco Blanco, thought to represent the A.D. 1054 supernova.

to study with techniques that included computer modeling, paleobotanical research, remote sensing, carbon-14 dating, and archeomagnetism. The archeologists hoped to answer many questions: Why did the Anasazi build here? What was their social organization and who were their leaders? How did they relate to the world beyond Chaco Canyon? What happened to the Chacoans? Why did they leave, and where did they go?

One of the researchers' first goals was to find out exactly how many archeological sites lay within the national monument's thirty-two square miles. Survey crews, walking the entire national monument, recorded 1,751 sites on carefully gridded maps. Since then, archeologists have located more than 3,600 sites within present, expanded park boundaries, only 1 percent of which have been excavated.

These sites range from massive Pueblo Bonito to scattered remains of fire hearths, from early Basketmaker pithouse dwellings to ceremonially wide stairs laboriously chopped into the canyon's cliffs. Researchers found an ancient set of garden tools, including hoes with blades made of stone or mountain sheep horn bound with sinew to cottonwood poles.

They found images pecked into cliffs along the canyon: petroglyphs of deer, spirals, even astronomical events. For instance, just below Peñasco Blanco, a pictograph apparently records an exceedingly rare event—the explosion of a supernova that Chinese astronomers also recorded in A.D. 1054. Atop the mesas researchers found rings of piled stones that may have been used as shrines or signal stations.

The decade of work, conducted by dozens of archeologists, students, and assistants associated with the Chaco Center, produced almost ten thousand pages of written information as well as thousands of maps and photographs. This staggering amount of information has revealed a much broader view of the Chacoan world, but also has revealed complexities that researchers are still struggling to unravel.

An obvious research target was the Chacoan road system. Navajos living near Chaco, the Wetherills, Neil Judd, and Gordon Vivian all knew about the broad paths that connected canyon great houses with those on the mesas. A new technique, remote sensing, allowed

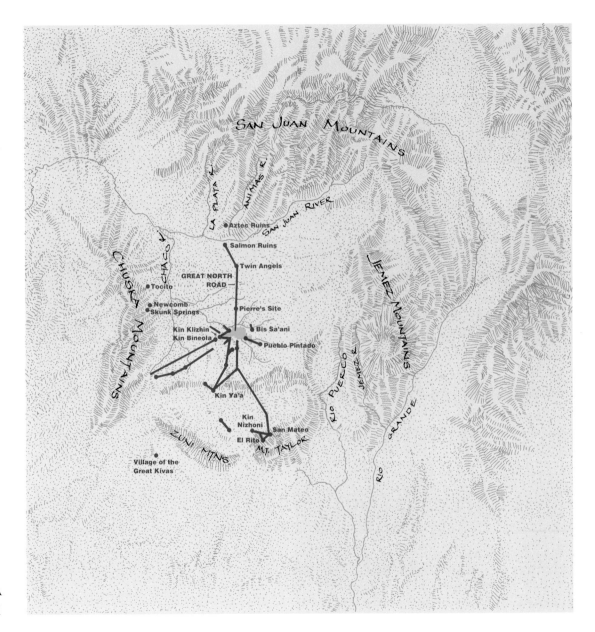

33

This lowlight, aerial photograph shows prehistoric roads converging at Pueblo Alto.

archeologists not only to see these roadways in relation to Chacoan structures, but also allowed them to plot their directions and lengths, much as one would plot a roadmap.

One type of remote sensing begins with low-level aerial photography, such as used by the United States Geological Survey. To give these two-dimensional photographs some depth, Chaco researchers employed a technique called stereoscopy, in which an object— a Chacoan great house, for example—

was photographed from two slightly different angles. The images were overlapped to give viewers a three-dimensional perspective of the subject. Researchers also used calibrated cameras that allowed them to translate a photograph into a computer graph. This technique, called photogrammetry, provided more precision in planning excavation strategies and analyzing structures.

Nonphotographic types of remote sensing also helped researchers. Radar

penetrated soil and rock in search of buried structures. Thermography (thermal infrared imagery) measured temperature differences between objects. Moist soils, for instance, radiate more heat than dry soils, allowing researchers to locate ancient irrigation ditches and roads. The roads that connect Chacoan great houses often lie a few centimeters lower than the surrounding land. Because the roadbeds are slightly lower, they collect more moisture, and can be picked out by thermography. More moisture also promotes the growth of more vegetation. Although difficult to spot on the ground, this plant density and the light reflected from it can be detected using remote-sensing photography.

Coordinating data, archeologists developed a map that showed roads radiating out from Chaco. Hundreds of miles of roads have been associated with the Chacoan culture, including more than a half dozen major routes. In general, the major routes are thirty feet wide, approximately the size of a modern two-lane road. Initially, archeologists were puzzled by the need for such wide roads, particularly when Chacoans had neither draft animals nor vehicles.

Chacoan roads are very nearly straight, suggesting that Chacoans had plotted the routes prior to building them, using line-of-sight engineering. Where realignments were required, Chacoan road builders corrected with "doglegs" rather than smooth curves. One oddity is the presence of parallel roads. The road system heading north contains two pairs of almost perfectly parallel roads. The roads in each pair are only fifty feet apart, and the pairs themselves are about one hundred feet apart.

Studying the roads close up, archeologists found that Chacoan road builders had scraped off the top layer of soil to expose a harder layer below. Often, the subsurface is caliche, formed when naturally occurring calcium carbonate binds sand and other material into a hard, cement-like substance. The removed soil likely was piled alongside the roadbeds to form berms, marking the road's edge. Where roads crossed slickrock, their edges were often bordered with piled-up rocks or rows of small boulders. If stone was readily available, low walls were often constructed along both sides of the road. Some of the best preserved walls are in

New Alto on the north mesa.

Evidence of prehistoric roadways can be seen at Kin Ya'a, south of Chaco Canyon.

the vicinity of Pueblo Alto.

The Pueblo Alto complex consists of the Pueblo Alto great house plus three smaller pueblos: New Alto, East Ruin, and Rabbit Ruin. The complex is criss-crossed with roads and gives every indication of being a major junction. Some of these roads lead out across the mesa, while others lead to stairways and ramps that connect the cliff tops with Chaco Canyon. At an opening in Pueblo Alto's north wall, four, perhaps five, roads converge. One of these, the so-called Great North Road, heads due north for more than thirty miles.

Chacoans began building these oversized, labor-intensive roads about the time their masonry reached its classic Bonito Phase, during the eleventh century. Archeologists determined road dates by analyzing ceramics found along the roads, because ceramics can be associated with absolute dates. Since almost every road is associated with an outlying Chacoan-style great house, if the outlier's beams and masonry styles can be dated, those dates could help date the associated road. A number of the larger outliers, such as Aztec Ruins, had been known to archeologists for decades, but they had been seen as

discrete units until the Chacoan road system helped tie them together. The search for roads led archeologists to previously unknown outlying great houses, while known outliers led them to new road segments. Occasionally the twentieth century intrudes, obscuring Chacoan road segments with pipelines or other development. Nevertheless, archeologists have discovered much of the Chacoan system. They have also discovered that, in many cases, outliers are spaced a day's journey along the routes, much like inns in American colonial times. Shrines and small ruins found on road segments between outliers and Chaco Canyon may have been used for signal-fire communications.

Roads lead south, southeast, and southwest, but the roads north tie the largest outliers into the Chaco network: Salmon Ruins, on the San Juan River, and Aztec Ruins, on the Animas River. Aztec Ruins, misnamed by early Anglo-American settlers, is a national monument in its own right, and contains the third-largest Bonito Phase building (after Pueblo Bonito and Chetro Ketl) and the only fully reconstructed great kiva extant.

So far, archeologists have discov-ered more than one hundred outlying great house structures, but that might be only half the total number scattered throughout the Colorado Plateau. Some archeologists believe this architectural phenomenon spread from the Rocky Mountains all the way to the Mogollon Rim, which separates the Colorado Plateau from Arizona's Sonoran Desert. Finding them all would prove difficult because few outliers are as massive and obvious as the great houses in Chaco Canyon. Many have been covered with the rubble of later occupations and the sediment of centuries.

Although a few outlier great houses, such as Aztec and Salmon ruins, had hundreds of rooms and rose three to four stories, most had less than fifty rooms and one or two stories. What defines these scattered ruins as Chacoan is their overall mass, distinctive core-and-veneer sandstone masonry, the horizontal patterns of the masonry, and the architecture of the kivas. Layout and construction was similar to that found in Chaco Canyon. And, like Chaco, most outliers had enclosed plazas.

Archeologists have found non-Chacoan architectural influences at the outliers as well. Some structures were built in the blocky McElmo style, reinforcing the belief that the Chacoan system was influenced, over time, by Anasazi from the Mesa Verde area.

Other community structures—roads, great kivas, and small houses—were also patterned on Chaco. At outliers, however, the large, central building and the small houses are more obviously integrated. As at Chaco, roads are associated with great houses and the great houses, in turn, help integrate all the community structures.

Water was a determining factor in siting outliers; many lie near drainages or springs so residents could employ floodwater or irrigation for farming. Apart from Chaco Canyon, the most well-watered areas lie near the mountains that rim the San Juan Basin. Newcomb, Skunk Springs, and Tocito all lie to the west, near the Chuska Mountains. Village of the Great Kivas is on Zuni Pueblo tribal land near the Zuni Mountains. Kin Nizhoni, El Rito, and San Mateo lie in a cluster near the foot of Mount Taylor, toward the southeast.

Many outliers are situated on prominent land forms, such as mesas and promontories. Prominent positions may have had something to do with defense—and communications. At the Pierre's Site outlier, for instance, archeologists have found evidence of fire-building atop a natural cone formation known as El Faro, the Lighthouse. Evidence of large fires at signal stations along the roads presents a picture of Anasazi travelers, trekking arrow-straight roads at night, always within sight of a signal fire to guide their way.

Certain outliers include tower kivas, which may have served still another purpose. Some archeologists believe that spatial configurations, especially astronomical alignments, were important to the Anasazi, as they were to many ancient peoples. Tower kivas, with their unobstructed views of the clear southwestern sky, might just as well have served as sky observatories as command towers.

Anasazi began constructing the early outlying great houses by the early tenth century, about the same time as Chacoan Anasazi were building Pueblo Bonito and Una Vida. By A.D. 1050, a building boom had begun throughout the Chacoan world. Road building, trade, great house construction both in the canyon and throughout the region all flourished during this period, much

as London and Paris were blossoming in medieval Europe at about the same period.

During the 1000s and early 1100s, Anasazi social organization was a large web of communities, reaching out from Chaco Canyon to include more than 90,000 square miles of the surrounding region and as many as 150 communities. Hundreds of miles of roads connected Chacoan communities, creating the only prehistoric, road-linked culture north of Mexico.

Yet, by 1140 the boom had ended. Some road segments had been used only fifty years; some outliers may have been used for only one or two generations. And the Chaco great houses were deserted. In order to understand what brought about this dramatic change, archeologists had to look more closely at how Chacoans lived.

One of the most important tasks was cultivation of the corn, squash, and beans that formed the base of the Anasazi diet. Unlike secular societies, in the Anasazi world daily life and religion were bound together and the cycle of the seasons was particularly important. Planting was done at the proper time with due ceremony given to the seeds

Casa Chiquita, once a
compact pueblo of about
50 rooms and 3 kivas.

▣ Chaco's Daily Occurrences

When faced with silent, austere ruins, it is sometimes hard to imagine a bustling, vital community. We see the shells of buildings, but we do not see the crops that dotted the canyon floor, the water-filled canals that irrigated the crops, the people who tended the crops or worked at any other of the myriad tasks that life in Chaco Canyon required.

As in agricultural societies all over the world, Chacoans probably rose early. A group of men and some of the older boys may have set off before sunrise with their hunting weapons, hoping to down some rabbits, perhaps a deer, before the heat of the day sent most animals seeking cover.

After the morning meal, builders might have returned to the work of the previous day—carefully laying courses of sandstone blocks on the latest addition to the pueblo. Others, and perhaps elders of the community—those too old to hunt or crack stone—would focus their attention on pottery. (The average Anasazi lifespan was about the same as anyone living a thousand years ago: thirty-five to fifty-five years.) Sitting on one of the pueblo's broad terraces, potters turned clay into a variety of shapes and sizes before painting and firing. A group of four or five women would work side by side in one of the covered mealing rooms, perhaps discussing children and the day's events. Surrounded by their families' outdoor chores, children would be free to play and to learn life skills by mimicking the work of their elders. Adding to the action were the community's domesticated dogs and turkeys.

and seedlings that would eventually sustain them.

Archeologists figured that an irrigation system was Chaco culture's answer to farming in an arid land, especially since they knew that other prehistoric peoples in the Southwest had practiced water control. Judd and other early archeologists had found evidence of irrigation canals and dams, but it took modern archeologists to confirm the extent and workings of these structures.

Gordon Vivian was the first to systematically study the irrigation systems that Neil Judd had suspected. His son, Gwinn, advanced the study of Chacoan fields, irrigation systems, and other structures by analyzing aerial photographs taken by the Soil Conservation Service in the 1930s. These images showed a section of ground near Chetro Ketl to be more sparsely vegetated than the surrounding land. The vegetation pattern formed an almost perfect rectangle. The twelve-acre rectangle, bordered by earthen-and-stone berms, was divided by canals into quadrants, each quadrant further divided by irrigation ditches into eighty-four small plots. Once planted in the

Arrows with stone points hafted onto wooden foreshafts.

clay soil, crops were nurtured with spring runoff and summer flash flood waters. The water was directed to gridded fields via a system of diversion dams, channels, and stone headgates.

To verify this finding, researchers scanned the garden area with an electric magnetometer, which measures soil density. Computer models, based on magnetometer data, indicated earthen berms just where aerial photographs showed them to be. That Chacoans used irrigation was clear; less clear was the source of their water.

Water in the Southwest appears capriciously. Occasional winter storms may produce snowcover, which can disappear quickly in the presence of sun and bone-dry air. Spring sees some rainfall, but by far the greatest amount of water comes from brief but violent late summer storms. During July and August, airy noontime clouds build to dark, towering thunderheads by mid-afternoon. When they burst, they can deluge the land with up to an inch of water in less than an hour. These storms rarely last long. Once clouds have dumped their loads, they dissipate, clearing the sky for rose-and-gold sunsets.

The hardpan earth cannot absorb much of these sudden deluges, so runoff rushes toward low places, cutting arroyos and washes such as Chaco Wash. To a certain extent, Anasazi and earlier Basketmaker societies depended on floodwaters from Chaco Wash to irrigate their crops. But irrigation canals that depended solely on Chaco Wash could not have supported a canyon peopled by thousands because its depth waxes and wanes. For decades Chaco Wash may be shallow, thus easily tapped by irrigation canals. Then, over a period of years, floodwaters may cut deeply into the canyon bottom, en-

trenching the wash as much as thirty feet, making it difficult to tap for irrigation. Eventually, the walls of the wash collapse, sediment builds up, and Chaco Wash once again becomes shallow.

Because the wash was always an inconsistent water source over the time that domestic, agricultural, and construction demands were at their peak, Gwinn Vivian looked for another water source—and found it. In the aftermath of a summer thunderstorm at Chaco, sheets of water stream across the mesas, running so quickly that little soaks in. When the water reaches the cliffs of Chaco Canyon, it explodes over the edges in dozens of waterfalls. The effect is breathtaking, an energetic life force in a dry land. Chacoan farmers found a way of capturing this runoff, and Vivian determined how they did it.

Rainfall that streams off the mesas first drops onto a slickrock bench more than a half-mile wide in some places. The runoff is funneled to low places along the bench where it splashes to the canyon floor below. The storm waters have eroded these areas, forming rincons, or little canyons, that punctuate the line of sheer rock walls along Chaco Canyon's north side.

Petroglyphs above Una Vida pueblo.

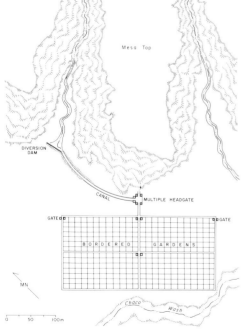

Chaco Wash after a summer thunderstorm.

Gwinn Vivian's map of water control system near Peñasco Blanco.

Most of Chaco's great houses are sited near these rincons or near Chaco's few side canyons, which also provide water drainage into the main canyon. Careful excavation showed that Chacoans built diversion dams at the mouths of the rincons to slow and channel runoff. A main canal then carried this water to a series of stone headgates, which could be opened to feed water into small ditches, evenly distributing water to garden plots separated by small, earthen ridges.

About two dozen water catchment areas occur along the north side of the canyon; many required considerable civic energy to build. For instance, the diversion dam at Cly Canyon, near Casa Chiquita, is 20 feet thick, 7 feet high and 120 feet long, with a 3.5-foot-wide gate in the middle to feed the water into a canal. The stone-lined canals averaged nine feet wide and two to five feet deep. Where canals could not easily be dug, Chacoans constructed masonry canal segments.

Water-control systems were laid out systematically along the entire north side of the canyon bottom, with water from each rincon flowing to a major section of gridded fields. Vivian estimates ten thousand individual garden plots may have been watered by irrigation. That would be enough, he believes, to support a population of five to six thousand.

While Gwinn Vivian was studying canals and roads, archeologists Thomas Windes and Stephen Lekson were further probing the great houses. They were determined to find out how rooms were used and organized, how each room fit into a system of family apartments, and how apartments and kivas fit into the whole pueblo.

Analyzing the progress of Chacoan culture depended on accurate dating techniques, and dendrochronology had become so sophisticated that scientists could determine the amount of annual precipitation from the width of each tree ring. They could even determine whether or not the log had been cut in the spring, when the wood was green. Of the estimated two hundred thousand pieces of wood used in constructing canyon great houses, only eight thousand or so have survived. All of these remaining pieces have been documented, 2,500 have been tested, and 1,200 have yielded dates.

In their efforts to analyze each

Interior rooms of Pueblo Bonito.

Archeologists locating prehistoric roads during the Chaco Project, 1972.

element of Chacoan construction, a few archeologists turned their attention to a representative section of Pueblo Alto. Pueblo Alto, a 133-room great house with numerous kivas but no great kiva, was constructed over a period of about 120 years. Construction began in A.D. 1020, when the culture was reaching its zenith, so Pueblo Alto may be indicative of the classic Chaco period.

The goal of present-day archeologists is to disturb as little of a site as possible, saving unexcavated ruins for future archeologists and posterity. Sophisticated tools now allow them to analyze much more while excavating much less. One of the most useful has been the computer, which allows archeologists to consolidate and interpret huge amounts of data in order to see patterns and create models for every aspect of Chacoan life.

Although they excavated only 10 percent of Pueblo Alto, archeologists have collected more data from that one section than from all the great houses in the decades before the Chaco Project. Based on their findings, archeologists figure a typical Chacoan household suite consisted of two rooms backed by two smaller storage rooms. Researchers

estimate that each household suite may have housed a family of five to ten people, including children, parents, and grandparents. Sometimes a corridor fronted these four-room suites, connecting the suites to each other and to the central plaza.

Room features included shallow firepits, stone-lined hearths, pot rests (a raised adobe ring or a depression in the floor), mealing bins, wall niches, and vents, which were almost always placed high in the walls. Few of these features,

**Potsherds from the
Chuska Valley found at
Pueblo Alto.**

which indicate daily use, were found in storage rooms. Doors were covered with slabs of rock or willow mats and, in general, those that led outside to the plaza had low thresholds while doorways between rooms were often set three feet or more above the floor to conserve heat.

Frigid mid-winter temperatures would have required firepits and hearths for heating as well as cooking. Thus, one test of population density in the pueblos is the number of firepits indicating that rooms or suites were used regularly. The sticking point is that archeologists have found very few household suites in the great houses: only five at Pueblo Alto, possibly as few as five at Pueblo Bonito, and no more than eleven at Una Vida.

What they have found are many large-room suites of as much as three hundred square feet—about twice the size of a household suite. Only 15 percent of the space was allocated for habitation, so these large-room suites may have been used ceremonially and only occasionally. Like early archeologists, present-day researchers were struck by the rarity of burials associated with great houses. This, together with the low number of room habitation features, throws the population count of Chaco Canyon into question.

Room analysis also revealed a high proportion of storage rooms to living quarters at Pueblo Alto. The exterior walls of Pueblo Alto were lined with rows of what researchers believe to be storage rooms. None of these rooms had access to Pueblo Alto's interior rooms, but each had an exterior door opening onto adjacent roads. Exterior doors on the backsides of great houses indicate that these rooms could have been road related. Perhaps they were meant for storing goods that came in from outlying communities.

Another sign of incoming goods is the number of pottery sherds found in a sample of the Pueblo Alto midden. Archeologists estimate the entire midden contains more than 150,000 broken pots—an extraordinary number. The average rate of use in a typical Anasazi village has been calculated to be about seventeen pots per family per year. The amount of sherds found in the Pueblo Alto midden would put the number of pots per Pueblo Alto family at 125. Each member of every family would have to be dangerously clumsy to require that many pots per year.

Researchers have identified about half of these vessels as ceramics from Chuska Valley outliers, thirty-seven miles to the west. No outbound traffic in pottery has been found that is at all proportionate to the numbers of vessels coming in to Pueblo Alto. Why would so much pottery have been brought to Chaco and so little have gone out? Although Chaco Project research raised many questions, archeologists were beginning to formulate some answers.

CHAPTER THREE

RELIGION & TRADE

Unlike many of today's societies, the Anasazi did not separate the concepts of religion and work. Religion was integral to all they did. In this land of little water, planting and harvesting corn—the Anasazi staff of life—required the cooperation of spiritual forces. Whereas now we can pump water from rivers hundreds of miles away, or dip deeply into aquifers hundreds of feet below the surface, Chacoans had to survive on a much more marginal level. Water, or the lack of it, defines desert cultures, and, to some extent, Chacoan culture can be charted according to fluctuations in precipitation. Some archeologists believe the peopling of the San Juan Basin was triggered by a climate change almost five hundred years before Pueblo Bonito was built. As the climate became cooler and moister, archeologists believe people moved down from the surrounding mountains to join Basketmaker peoples already dwelling in Chaco and other areas of the San Juan Basin.

The late eighth century saw the beginning of a warming and drying trend. Archeologists postulate that, this

A "small house" on the south side of Chaco Canyon.

Pueblo Bonito, largest great house on the north side of the canyon.

time, Basketmaker peoples responded by adapting to their environment rather than moving to wetter areas. They intensified their agricultural efforts with irrigation and simple brush dams, thus creating surpluses and the need for storage structures.

By the tenth century, the climate had changed again, this time becoming wetter. In the San Juan Basin, wetter may mean an inch or two more precipitation per year, but a few inches at the right time can make a huge difference. Dating techniques show that the tenth century was the wettest in a thousand years. Again, people responded, this time with a building boom that would span almost three centuries.

Although Pueblo Bonito began modestly enough in the ninth century, over the years its builders created a much grander structure. No one knows exactly why building styles changed, but some speculate that societal classes began to develop. Farmers who became more successful may have decided to build bigger houses to trumpet their wealth and success—not an uncommon trait in most societies. A priestly class may have developed. Some archeologists believe two societies may have blossomed simultaneously in Chaco Canyon: great house builders representing Anasazi from the north, near Mesa Verde, and villagers representing southern Anasazi, whose small-house groupings line the south side of the canyon.

However Chacoan society grew, archeologists agree that hierarchies developed. Among the few burials found in the great houses some revealed a wealth of jewelry, decorated ceremonial staffs, and effigies inlaid with turquoise and shells. Burials uncovered in south-side villages were far simpler and without the trappings of wealth. Although Chacoan society probably was divided into different classes, there are no indications that a slave class existed.

Chacoan culture reached its peak from the early tenth to the mid-twelfth centuries. After that, the Anasazi began deserting the canyon, but the Anasazi themselves did not disappear. They merely moved on, evolving into the contemporary Puebloan peoples of the Southwest.

Chacoan architecture, represented by Pueblo Bonito, began with a larger version of the pueblo village model and

Corner door in Pueblo Bonito, aligned with the winter solstice sunrise.

Distinctive light patterns are formed by architectural alignments during solstices and equinoxes.

grew to include multistoried buildings with storehouses, living quarters, plazas, and kivas of every sort. Chacoans planned buildings and additions, laying out elaborate foundations in advance. Great houses were usually sited facing southeast, serving as huge solar collectors to warm the pueblo in winter. Doors and vent systems were built with temperature control in mind.

Because their diets were based on corn, Chacoans also were attuned to the sun's yearly course, equinoxes, solstices and, especially, when to plant. Some archeologists believe Chacoans incorporated this astronomical knowledge into their structures as well as into their lives.

In certain Puebloan tribes, such as the Zuni Pueblo, religious leaders are charged with keeping the calendar. They have developed a system in which the angle of the sun shining through particular windows highlights calibrated lines on a wall, alerting them to crucial points in the seasons. It may be that such astronomical systems were passed down from Anasazi times.

Probably the most famous of Chacoan archeoastronomical markers is the so-called Sun Dagger, found high

on a shoulder of Fajada Butte on the southeastern floor of the canyon. Three vertical slabs of sandstone, which fell from the top of the butte centuries ago, are aligned in such a way that a thin "dagger" of sunlight pierces the cliff face at noon each day. There, Anasazis carved two spirals into the rock. At approximately noon on the summer solstice, the light of the Sun Dagger falls on the middle of the larger spiral. At the winter solstice, two shafts of light bracket the outer edges of that spiral. At spring and autumn equinoxes, a smaller shaft of light bisects the smaller spiral. A slab has shifted, however, possibly due to a combination of natural events and human traffic. To protect this fragile place, visitor access to Fajada Butte has been restricted.

Lines projected from the exterior walls of Pueblo Bonito, Pueblo del Arroyo, and other great houses converge too often and in ways too significant to be coincidental. Some archeologists say it is more than mere chance that Tsin Kletsin on South Mesa, the great kiva Casa Rinconada, and Pueblo Alto on Alto Mesa line up with each other on a true north-south alignment. Assuming these complex

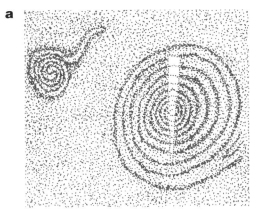

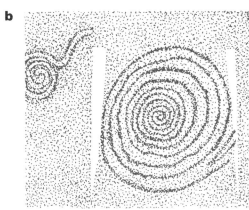

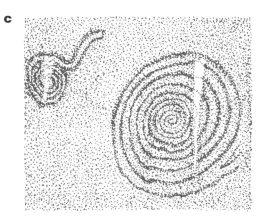

The summer solstice (a), winter solstice (b), and equinoxes (c) as indicated by the Sun Dagger on Fajada Butte.

mathematical alignments were planned, they show a very human need on the part of Chacoans to create order in the world around them.

Undoubtedly, the edifices that Chacoans erected served some of the same purposes as the great edifices being erected in medieval Europe or Mesoamerica during the same period. Notre Dame, Paris' magnificent gothic cathedral, was begun in the twelfth century. The capitals of Toltec and late Mayan civilizations, which thrived about the same time as Chacoan culture, centered on dramatic stepped pyramids that were meant to instill the same sense of importance as Pueblo Bonito.

Societies of a thousand years ago, whether in Europe or the Americas, were not as compartmentalized as today's western societies. Today, houses of worship, stores, and government buildings are separate. In Anasazi society (and in contemporary Puebloan societies), religion, commerce, and urban administration often occurred in the same complex. In fact, many archeologists now think that great houses were more societal centers than living quarters. Rather than crammed with people, like so many prehistoric apartment buildings, great houses may have been inhabited only at certain times of the year. Their main functions may have been to serve as impressive monuments and meeting places.

Archeologists generally agree on estimates of the number of Chacoans living in the villages along the south cliffs. But a number of archeologists now believe that the great houses were populated mainly by an elite and a few caretakers. They cite the lack of burials, hearths and firepits, or other signs of daily habitation as evidence that great houses were used occasionally for ceremonial and religious events.

The great houses, they say, were significant and served the religious and political needs of many people, but few people lived in them. The buildings were a spiritual and material expression of the culture and became focal points, binding people more closely to the culture.

As the architecture of Chaco Canyon grew more complex so did the means for supplying raw materials. When Chacoans used up nearby stands of timber for construction and heating, they had to trek to forests on the mountainous edges of the San Juan Basin.

Lugging beams up to two feet in diameter and as much as twelve feet long must have required extraordinary effort. A present-day mathematician has proposed a way Chacoans could have transported lumber: Door lintels in Chaco great houses are logs about four feet long; ten men lined up in pairs might have managed to support a roof beam atop five lintels, one lintel carried by each pair, thus distributing the beam's weight. Not an easy four- to five-day walk from the Chuska Mountains, but manageable.

Building a culture in the desert required constant adaptation. The year 1026 saw the beginning of a twenty-five-year drought, during which resources probably became strained and groups of people may have begun moving out of Chaco Canyon. At about this time, intensive building of roads and outliers began. Archeologists speculate that by spreading population centers to outliers, yet retaining Chaco as the cultural center, the Anasazi may have tried to keep Chacoan culture from collapsing amid the drought.

Making the roads ceremonially wide and lining them with stones and walls near the entrances to Chaco Canyon

would help to impress outlying populations with the grandeur and continued importance of Chaco Canyon great houses and leaders. Thus, the roads were tangible and symbolic, like the impressively wide boulevards of Washington, D.C., and the Champs Elysee in Paris.

Archeologists know that trade existed. Since hunter-gatherer times, mobility was a survival mechanism. Despite the fact that foot travel was difficult, prehistoric peoples of the Southwest and Mesoamerica were quite mobile, both in terms of migrations and trade. The Southwest alone was full of peoples with whom Chacoan Anasazi could have traded: Mogollon and Hohokam to the south and the Hakataya around the Grand Canyon, among others. And, of course, Anasazi settlements themselves ranged beyond the San Juan Basin, covering much of the Colorado Plateau.

Trade with Mesoamerican city-states brought to Chaco macaws, copper bells, seashells, and perhaps architectural styles such as the covered colonnade at Chetro Ketl. Mesoamerican cultures were particularly interested in a trade item that they could have gotten in large quantities from Anasazi regions: turquoise, ubiquitous in Mesoamerican jewelry, shields, masks, and other artifacts.

Turquoise may have been mined at Cerillos and other sites in the Southwest, but it was processed into beads, pendants, and other forms elsewhere in the region. Some archeologists believe turquoise may have been a medium of intercultural trade, with Chaco as "the mint." Evidence of turquoise processing is found in some of the great houses and villages along the south side of the canyon, where about a quarter of a million pieces of turquoise have been excavated.

One controversial idea posits that Chaco also may have served as the center of a huge redistribution network.

Because climate can be extremely local, it might have been effective to spread population centers around the basin. That way, the Anasazi could hedge their bets on rainfall and crop survival. Surplus corn or squash at one outlier could have been brought to Chaco, stored, then redistributed within Chaco Canyon or to outlying populations that did not reap such a good harvest.

The concept of Chaco as a regional distribution center has become shakier,

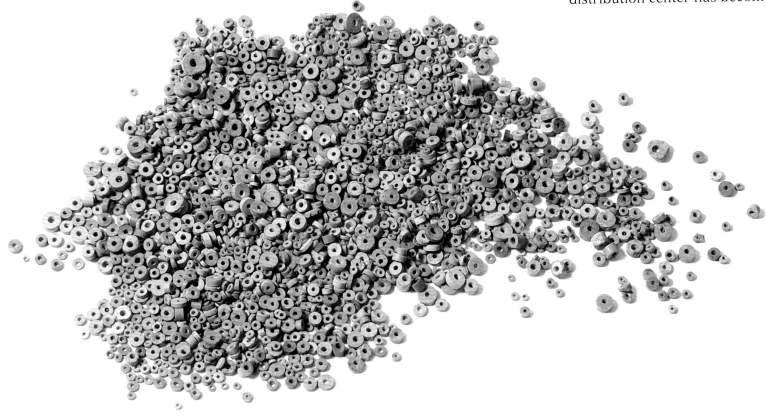

Cache of turquoise beads found in Pueblo Bonito.

however, as archeologists learn more. Pottery trade between Chaco Canyon and outliers is fairly easy to trace because clays and tempering materials can be linked to specific points of origin. Excavations have yielded black-on-white ware from the Red Mesa Valley south of Chaco, and corrugated ceramics from the Chuska Valley to the west, as well as pottery from other outlying areas.

Many kinds of ceramics came into Chaco Canyon, but there is little evidence that canyon dwellers redistributed any of these items to the outliers. On the contrary, those studying Pueblo Alto believe that the tens of thousands of smashed vessels—as well as enormous amounts of discarded lithics—found in the Pueblo Alto midden may have been brought to Chaco for the express purpose of being ritually broken.

Although probably not a redistribution center, Chaco may have been the administrative and religious center of a larger Anasazi world. Imbued with importance, rather than populated with residents, Chetro Ketl and other great houses may have been the objects of pilgrimages, such as Canterbury,

England, was at about the same time. It may be that groups from the outliers made pilgrimages to Chaco at planting time, the fall equinox, the winter solstice, and other times during the year. When they arrived at Chaco, each group may have stayed together in one of the large-room suites found throughout the great houses.

If Chacoan great houses were religious and administrative centers, rather than dwelling places, laboring to build them may have been a privileged act of faith and devotion. Archeologists have estimated that it would have taken thirty men ten years, working two to four months a year, to complete a major Chacoan construction project, such as a large addition to a great house.

If permanent residents at any great house amounted to dozens rather than hundreds, population overload at Chaco Canyon and mass migrations to the outliers becomes a less plausible explanation for the demise of Chaco as a cultural center. Then why move the center of the Anasazi world from Chaco in the mid-twelfth century?

Perhaps a few seasons of crop failures alerted leaders that Chaco Canyon was no longer a propitious

place. But archeologists point out that when societies make major changes, those changes are based on a number of factors, even though one factor may seem outstanding. By the end of the eleventh century and the beginning of the twelfth century, life in Chacoan culture was changing rapidly. Most obvious is the change in architecture, from classic Bonito style to the compact McElmo style.

Resources within Chaco Canyon, from quarried stone to firewood to wildlife, may have become depleted from overuse. During this period the amount of deer bones in trash middens decreased and the numbers of small-mammal remains rose. By A.D. 1120, Chacoan construction using new wood had ended. By 1130, a fifty-year drought had set in. By 1150, the great houses of Chaco Canyon were practically deserted.

Though migration was part of the way of life for Anasazi and many other prehistoric peoples, the demise of Chaco Canyon as the center of Anasazi cultural and religious life cannot be viewed as a mass migration. For one, small-house construction and reuse continued sporadically. Those who left the canyon probably left in stages, over

▣ Classic Chaco Masonry

Pueblo Bonito's oldest walls, Type I, are a single width of shaped sandstone slabs, thickly mortared and plastered with mud. Originally, many thousands of small sandstone fragments, or spalls, were pressed into the plaster that covered some Type I walls. This spall-studded plaster was meant to protect the load-bearing masonry and served as a true veneer. Unfortunately, most of Pueblo Bonito's spall-studded veneer has been lost through erosion.

At least three other styles of masonry found within Chaco Canyon were unique within the Anasazi world and are the hallmark of Chacoan architecture, whether the building lies within the canyon or anywhere else in the region.

Chacoan-style masonry, what Judd called Bonito Phase, consists of an inner and outer wall with rubble filling the space in between. This "core-and-veneer" style was much more stable than single-thickness masonry and provided better insulation. Such walls also could support multiple stories because they could be built wide at the base and tapered to the top to distribute the load efficiently.

Type II, the first of this core-and-veneer masonry that Judd classified, used dressed sandstone slabs of uniform size, laid without much symmetry. Small chips of sandstone filled the spaces around the larger blocks.

Type III used uniformly cut and

dressed sandstone blocks laid in bands that alternated with smaller tabular pieces. Type IV, the most sophisticated-looking of Bonito Phase masonry, used uniformly cut and dressed sandstone pieces throughout. These pieces were laid symmetrically, often in subtle patterns.

Pueblo del Arroyo with
its unusual tri-walled
structure.

a generation or two. As ceremonial and administrative centers, the great houses may not have supported huge populations anyway.

The world has seen civilizations come and go. Hundreds, perhaps thousands, of prehistoric cultures lived, flourished, and ebbed without much notice. For instance, Teotihuacan was one of the largest early settlements in the world, a city-state of great pyramids and art located in the Valley of Mexico. In the sixth century A.D., almost a quarter of a million people lived there. (At the time, London was populated by only a few tens of thousands.) Yet, by the ninth century, Teotihuacan was no more, and few besides archeologists now recognize its name. A hundred years after Chaco Canyon was abandoned, the Aztec civilization emerged in what is now Mexico. Like Chacoan culture, it lasted about 250 years.

Although Chacoan culture rose and fell almost a millennium ago, what happened in Chaco Canyon is noteworthy. Prehistoric peoples, the Anasazi, took the crucial first steps beyond existence as a loose aggregation of agricultural communities toward a complex society. Viewed from the perspective of modern times, Chacoan culture flourished for longer than the United States has existed as a nation.

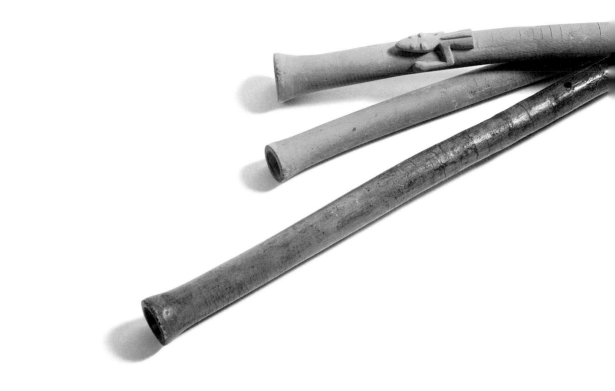

Flutes, one with carved lizard head, discovered in Pueblo Bonito.

**Migration of the Anasazi
after 1300.**

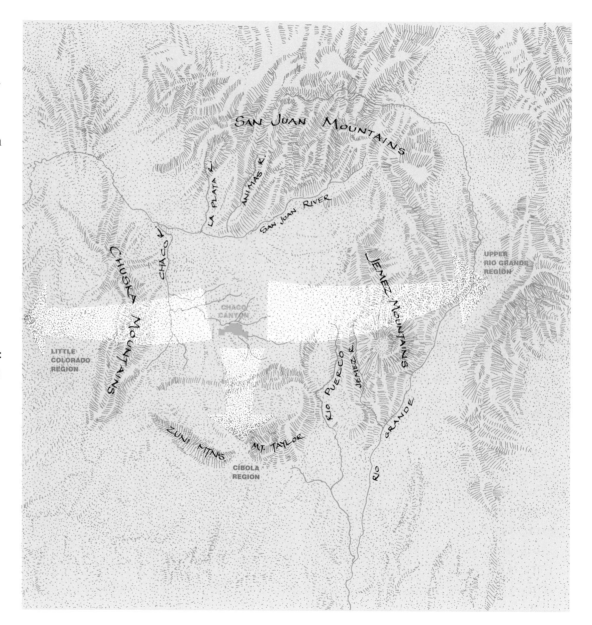

Although Chaco Canyon was abandoned as an Anasazi cultural center in the mid-1100s, Anasazi history did not end. The center moved north. Migration stories are central to the spiritual life of Puebloan peoples and probably were to their ancestors, the Anasazi. Directions, too, are an important part of the Puebloan world view. Interestingly, north, the direction the Anasazi migrated after Chaco, is seen by some Puebloan communities as the direction of birth and death.

The Great North Road leading from Chaco points to the next Anasazi center: Aztec Ruins, on the banks of the Animas River at the foot of the San Juan Mountains. Aztec Ruins National Monument, located near the border of New Mexico and Colorado, includes twenty-seven acres of ruins, most of them unexcavated. The largest of those excavated, West Ruin, rose three stories and contained about four hundred rooms plus a dozen kivas, including a great kiva. West Ruin, completed in 1115 before Chaco was abandoned, is clearly a Chacoan great house. They knew where they would move and had built the next center.

But Aztec Ruins did not last long as an Anasazi center, nor was it the only one. Regional centers had been developing across the Colorado Plateau: in the La Plata River Valley, near the Chuska Mountains, and elsewhere. By the late twelfth century, Montezuma Valley, just west of Mesa Verde in what is now southwestern Colorado, became a focal point. Mesa Verdean Anasazi had lived in Montezuma Valley for centuries, and by 1200 they had built a dozen or so great houses whose size rivals those at Chaco Canyon. Few of these have been excavated, but archeologists know that by the fourteenth century they, too, were abandoned.

Again, archeologists cannot point to any one explanation for abandoning regional centers such as Montezuma Valley. A severe, twenty-year drought began in 1276, but depleted resources, erosion, and a society too complex for its environmental situation may all have been factors.

Beginning about 1300, the Anasazi departed the entire region, an exodus astonishing in its totality. Anasazi regional centers, such as Chaco and Aztec Ruins, no longer functioned after 1300. Instead, the Anasazi of what is now called the Four Corners region moved south, west, and east. There they joined others who already lived on the Hopi mesas and along the Chama and Little Colorado rivers, the Rio Puerco, and the Rio Grande near present-day Santa Fe and Albuquerque.

Although cultural influences may have continued to shift easily among Puebloans, as they did in the days of their ancestors the Anasazi, after 1300 Puebloan communities began functioning more as autonomous units. Today, because of land tenure laws and other outside influences, the pueblos are distinct: Zuni, Zia, Acoma, Hopi, Jemez, and Santa Domingo, among others.

By the fifteenth century, Athabaskan-speaking people—Navajos and Apaches—had moved to the Colorado Plateau from the north. In general, the Navajo Nation proved highly adaptive, and is especially integral to the history of Chaco Canyon after its abandonment as an Anasazi center. Navajos learned agricultural methods from Puebloan people still in the area and later adopted horses and metal tools from the Span-ish. Their numbers grew in the San Juan Basin and throughout the region.

The sixteenth century saw the arrival of another new people, who changed life in the Southwest irrevocably. In April of 1540, Spanish conquistador Francisco Vásquez de Coronado and a huge expedition set out from what is now Mexico. They had heard reports of the wealth of Cíbola (Zuni) to the north. The Zunis challenged the Spanish, but were conquered and subjugated.

Finding none of the fabled riches, the Spanish ventured farther, to the Hopi mesas and the pueblos of Acoma and the Rio Grande Valley. Intolerant of Puebloan religions, they started missions and tried to convert native peoples to the Roman Catholic faith and Spanish culture. Conversion to Roman Catholicism and suppression of Kachina cults and other Puebloan beliefs went hand in hand. The Spanish also organized slave trade and stripped the area of resources, which they sent south.

Although the Spaniards had a reputation as fierce conquerors, their diseases were fiercer still. Some archeologists believe European diseases such as smallpox played a major role in Spanish conquests because native peoples, who had no immunity to these diseases, were devastated by them.

The coming of the Spanish created alliances and shifting relations among native peoples. Because Navajos lived in more dispersed and smaller settlements than Puebloans in the Rio Grande Valley and elsewhere, they generally remained free while the Spanish subdued the Puebloans. Fleeing the Spanish, many sought refuge among Navajo communities at the northeast edge of the San Juan Basin.

After more than a century of political and religious subjugation, native peoples had had enough. Although both Navajos and Puebloans desired political freedom, the religious issue was particularly important for the Puebloans because their spiritual life was so much a part of their tribal organization and daily life. While Spanish military strength in New Mexico had declined to a few hundred, Puebloan tribal strength had quietly grown. In 1680, the tribes united and, with a combined force of six thousand warriors, they defeated the Spanish.

Factional disputes eventually undermined Puebloan unity, and in 1692 the

Acoma, one of the oldest continually inhabited towns in North America.

In 1864, many Navajos were exiled to Fort Sumner.

Spanish returned in force to reconquer them. Again, Puebloans sought refuge with Navajos in the wilder parts of the Colorado Plateau, including the area around Chaco Canyon. The cultural distinctions became blurred. Although Navajos adopted much of the Puebloan material culture and rich cultural traditions, Puebloan refugees became subsumed in the growing Navajo community.

Struggles with the Spanish continued. Utes who had traveled down from the northern mountains captured Navajo and Puebloan slaves whom they sold to the Spanish. Navajos began settling in what was probably one of the safest areas, the middle of the San Juan Basin. By the mid-eighteenth century some Navajo communities had settled on Chacra Mesa, overlooking Chaco Canyon. There they evaded capture, but not the 1781 smallpox epidemic that decimated Puebloan and Navajo populations throughout New Mexico.

In 1821, as part of Mexico, the region won independence from Spain. In the 1820s, a Mexican-led incursion against the Navajos took them near Chaco Canyon and established a major military route into Navajo country. In

1849, a few years after the United States won the region from Mexico, a United States military expedition against the Navajos followed the same route, and it was during this expedition that Lieutenant James Simpson recorded the grandeur of Chaco's Anasazi ruins.

Increasingly, people of European descent were moving into this part of the Southwest, and Navajos were viewed as hostile. So, in 1864 the United States Army rounded up most Navajos, including those at Chaco, and marched them to exile at Fort Sumner in eastern New Mexico. Although they were allowed to return to their lands four years later, the next decade saw rising tensions as Hispanic and Anglo-American ranchers and homesteaders moved farther into the San Juan Basin. The newcomers brought in large herds of livestock and started towns such as Rosa and Bloomfield near Aztec Ruins. When the Hyde-Wetherill expedition arrived in Chaco in the mid-1890s, they found both Navajo and Hispanic sheepherders living on the mesas and in the canyon.

Although Chaco Canyon was designated a national monument in 1907, five years before New Mexico gained state-

Traditional Navajo economy centered on raising sheep and goats.

Archeologists engaged Navajos in excavation, as shown here during the Hyde expedition in 1896.

hood, the land had few protections. Land rights were confusing and ill-defined and, as other parts of the Basin became overgrazed, Anglo-American homesteaders and ranchers encroached on the Chaco Canyon area. During this period, the federal government began a program to control overgrazing in the Southwest by reducing native herds. This program affected Navajos living in and near Chaco Canyon, but did not apply to Hispanic and Anglo-American stockowners. One stockowner, wealthy and politically connected, brought huge numbers of sheep—some say sixty thousand head—into the canyon.

As ranchers took control of more acreage, Navajo grazing lands shrank and many found work with the archeological expeditions that came into Chaco Canyon, beginning with the Wetherill and Hyde expedition. Hostilities over grazing lands became increasingly volatile and Chacoan ruins increasingly threatened. Finally, in 1946 the National Park Service fenced park boundaries and eliminated all livestock from the park.

Since 1947 the National Park Service has overseen all archeological work done at Chaco. Gordon Vivian, the park's first official archeologist, began projects to stabilize canyon ruins even earlier, and hired Navajos for this preservation work. Navajos have been an integral part of the staff at Chaco ever since.

For at least three hundred years the Navajo Nation has been associated with Chaco Canyon, and during that time it has built a rich history that includes bloodlines and customs of Chaco Canyon's original settlers, the Anasazi. Puebloan peoples, too, still have ties to the culture that flourished in Chaco Canyon. The buildings at Acoma and other pueblos resonate with Anasazi forms. The spiritual life of Puebloan peoples is not shaped by the sharp-edged religious boundaries of the twentieth century, but is more akin to the seamless spirituality of their Anasazi ancestors.

As a place that tells part of the story of human history, Chaco Canyon is important to us all. In 1980, when Congress realized that energy exploration and development were threatening significant Chacoan outliers, it expanded park boundaries to protect a number of them, such as Kin Bineola and Kin Ya'a. At the same time, Congress changed

the park's designation from national monument to Chaco Culture National Historical Park.

In 1987, the park was designated a World Heritage site, one of only a dozen or so in the United States. The World Heritage program is a means by which the international community can preserve the finest works of nature and humanity for future generations. Other World Heritage sites, chosen because of their unique and significant contributions to the world's natural and cultural legacy, include the Galapagos Islands, the Serengeti Plain, and the Incas' Machu Picchu.

Chaco's ruins are unsurpassed in the United States and represent the apex of pre-Columbian Puebloan civilization. Here we can learn how one prehistoric group developed. But Chaco may also be a paradigm, informing us on many levels. The Anasazi world grew from a collection of simple farming communities to a society complete with central government, hierarchical administration, civic projects, and other aspects of a complex civilization. Then the Anasazi turned aside from those levels of complexity.

Perhaps in such an exacting envi-

ronment, there are limits to growth. Possibly, because of a long stretch of forgiving climatic conditions, Chacoans overstepped those limits, eventually adjusting by breaking into smaller groups. Maybe, in some situations, growing to ultimate complexity is the wrong choice, the less adaptive choice. In that case, maybe the Anasazi chose the right course for survival by simplifying society so they could persevere through the centuries. The fact that the Anasazi legacy lives on among Puebloan peoples, when so many other societies have become extinct, may be the best measure of success.

Sometimes, standing before Pueblo Bonito at dusk, the canyon is so still you can hear the rhythmic beat of a raven's wings as they stroke through the air. The great walls of the pueblo glow deep red in the light of the setting sun. Although it has stood silent for nearly eight centuries, Pueblo Bonito still has the power to impress. Looking around at Chetro Ketl just east and Pueblo del Arroyo across the way, we are reminded that Chacoan culture was a glorious burst of human achievement.

◪ Chaco Place Names

No one knows what names the builders gave the great houses, and perhaps no one ever will. Most of the names now used to describe each of the ruins derive from one of three cultures: Spanish, Navajo, or Puebloan. In fact, many Chacoan places have more than one name—some in more than one language.

Casa Chiquita means "little house" in Spanish. One of Casa Chiquita's Navajo names has the same meaning.

Casa Rinconada means "house where the canyons meet" in Spanish.

Chaco Canyon/Chacra Mesa: It is thought that both "chaco" and "chacra" were derived from Navajo meaning "white rock."

Chetro Ketl—the meaning and language of the name is lost to us. Carravahal, Lt. Simpson's guide during the Army's 1849 expedition, said Chetro Ketl meant "rain pueblo." One of Chetro Ketl's Navajo names means "house in the corner."

Fajada Butte means "banded butte" in Spanish, probably for the dark seam of coal that can be seen midway up the butte.

Hungo Pavi may be related to the Hopi name, Reed Spring Village, the oldest and one of the largest Hopi villages, established in the thirteenth century about 160 miles west of Chaco.

Kin Bineola is from the Navajo, meaning "house in which the wind swirls."

Kin Kletso is Navajo for "yellow house," describing the color of its sandstone masonry blocks.

Kin Klizhin is Navajo for "black house" because of the darker color of its masonry.

Kin Ya'a means "house rising up high" in Navajo.

Peñasco Blanco means "white cliff" in Spanish, probably for a light-colored bluff north of the great house.

Pueblo Bonito means "pretty village" in Spanish. A Navajo name for Pueblo Bonito means "house where the rocks are propped up," for the masonry and timbers the Navajos found reinforcing the bottom of Threatening Rock, which, despite these efforts, crashed down upon Pueblo Bonito in 1941.

Pueblo del Arroyo is Spanish for "village by the wash." It may be a translation of the Navajo name, which has a similar meaning.

Pueblo Pintado means "painted village" in Spanish. That name conjures a much prettier picture than one of its other names: Pueblo de los Ratones, "village of the mice."

Shabik'eshchee comes from a Navajo name for a petroglyph symbolizing the sun that was found on a rock near the ruin.

Tsin Kletzin is from the Navajo for "charcoal place," perhaps because of the charred timbers found there.

Una Vida means "one life" in Spanish. One of its Navajo names, based a witchcraft legend, means "house of the woman who makes you thin by starving you."

Wijiji is from the Navajo for "greasewood," the shrub that dominates the floor of Chaco Canyon.